# "HELP!
# I JUST FOUND OUT
# I'M A PIG!"

# "HELP! I JUST FOUND OUT I'M A PIG!"

*by Donald M. Klein*

*Illustrated by Ed Renfro*

Workman Publishing
New York

# *To my favorite Snake, Pig, and Dog.*

Library of Congress Cataloging in Publication Data

Klein, Donald.
    Help! I just found out I'm a pig.

    1. Astrology, Chinese—Anecdotes, facetiae, satire,
etc. I. Renfro, Ed II. Title.
PN6231.A73K5    1984    818'.5402    83-40532
        ISBN   0-89480-672-6

Cover illustration by Ed Renfro

. Workman Publishing Company, Inc.
1 West 39th Street
New York, N.Y. 10018

Manufactured in the United States of America
First Printing April 1984

10   9   8   7   6   5   4   3   2   1

# CONTENTS

# A LITTLE BACKGROUND

In the sixties the big craze was to introduce yourself to someone by saying, "Hi! What's your sign?" The response usually went something like "Wow, man, like I'm a Taurus. What's yours?" Mercifully, those days are over. But they did spawn worldwide interest in astrology which continues today. And as people learned more about horoscopes, they began to discover that the signs of the zodiac were only *half* the story... the *western* half. Long before the hippies were singing about Jupiter aligning with Mars, the Chinese were developing elaborate "destiny charts" and "compatibility charts" that enabled them to predict the future and plan accordingly. At the foundation of Oriental astrology lies the concept of horoscopes based on animal characteristics, and that's what this book is all about.

Legend has it that a few thousand years ago Buddha was sitting around with nothing to do, when he decided to call a meeting of all the animals in the world. It was supposed to be quite an event . . . a real dog and pony show, if you will. Although Buddha promised to make it worth everyone's while to attend, only twelve animals showed up. (You would think that after the Noah's Ark Affair most animals wouldn't risk snubbing a divine invitation, but some animals never learn.) Buddha was a little upset by the weak turnout, but he was a god of his word and rewarded the animals who *did* show up by devoting an entire year to each. The animals were very proud and happy, because in addition to having years named in their honor, Buddha arranged that all humans born in any given year took on some of the physical and emotional characteristics of the animal to whom that year is dedicated.

# WHICH ANIMAL ARE YOU?

The first step toward animal horoscope enlightenment is figuring out which animal sign you were born under. This is easy to do and requires only two things: knowledge of the day you were born and the ability to read the charts on the next pages. So, before you go further, take a few moments to find your sign.

After you discover which animal you *are,* you'll find out what you are *like.*

# THE YEARS OF THE PIG

| | | |
|---|---|---|
| JANUARY  30, 1911 | *to* | FEBRUARY 17, 1912 |
| FEBRUARY 16, 1923 | *to* | FEBRUARY  4, 1924 |
| FEBRUARY  4, 1935 | *to* | JANUARY  23, 1936 |
| JANUARY  22, 1947 | *to* | FEBRUARY  9, 1948 |
| FEBRUARY  8, 1959 | *to* | JANUARY  27, 1960 |
| JANUARY  27, 1971 | *to* | JANUARY  15, 1972 |
| FEBRUARY 13, 1983 | *to* | FEBRUARY  1, 1984 |
| JANUARY  31, 1995 | *to* | FEBRUARY 18, 1996 |

# THE YEARS OF THE RAT

| | | |
|---|---|---|
| JANUARY  31, 1900 | *to* | FEBRUARY 18, 1901 |
| FEBRUARY 18, 1912 | *to* | FEBRUARY  5, 1913 |
| FEBRUARY  5, 1924 | *to* | JANUARY  24, 1925 |
| JANUARY  24, 1936 | *to* | FEBRUARY 10, 1937 |
| FEBRUARY 10, 1948 | *to* | JANUARY  28, 1949 |
| JANUARY  28, 1960 | *to* | FEBRUARY 14, 1961 |
| FEBRUARY 15, 1972 | *to* | FEBRUARY  2, 1973 |
| FEBRUARY  2, 1984 | *to* | FEBRUARY 19, 1985 |

# THE YEARS OF THE BULL

| | | |
|---|---|---|
| FEBRUARY 19, 1901 | *to* | FEBRUARY  7, 1902 |
| FEBRUARY  6, 1913 | *to* | JANUARY  25, 1914 |
| JANUARY  25, 1925 | *to* | FEBRUARY 12, 1926 |
| FEBRUARY 11, 1937 | *to* | JANUARY  30, 1938 |
| JANUARY  29, 1949 | *to* | FEBRUARY 16, 1950 |
| FEBRUARY 15, 1961 | *to* | FEBRUARY  4, 1962 |
| FEBRUARY  3, 1973 | *to* | JANUARY  22, 1974 |
| FEBRUARY 20, 1985 | *to* | FEBRUARY  8, 1986 |

# THE YEARS OF THE TIGER

| | | |
|---|---|---|
| FEBRUARY 8, 1902 | to | JANUARY 28, 1903 |
| JANUARY 26, 1914 | to | FEBRUARY 13, 1915 |
| FEBRUARY 13, 1926 | to | FEBRUARY 1, 1927 |
| JANUARY 31, 1938 | to | FEBRUARY 18, 1939 |
| FEBRUARY 17, 1950 | to | FEBRUARY 5, 1951 |
| FEBRUARY 5, 1962 | to | JANUARY 24, 1963 |
| JANUARY 23, 1974 | to | FEBRUARY 10, 1975 |
| FEBRUARY 9, 1986 | to | JANUARY 28, 1987 |

## THE YEARS OF THE CAT

| | | |
|---|---|---|
| JANUARY 29, 1903 | to | FEBRUARY 15, 1904 |
| FEBRUARY 14, 1915 | to | FEBRUARY 2, 1916 |
| FEBRUARY 2, 1927 | to | JANUARY 22, 1928 |
| FEBRUARY 19, 1939 | to | FEBRUARY 7, 1940 |
| FEBRUARY 6, 1951 | to | JANUARY 26, 1952 |
| JANUARY 25, 1963 | to | FEBRUARY 12, 1964 |
| FEBRUARY 11, 1975 | to | JANUARY 30, 1976 |
| JANUARY 29, 1987 | to | FEBRUARY 16, 1988 |

## THE YEARS OF THE DRAGON

| | | |
|---|---|---|
| FEBRUARY 16, 1904 | to | FEBRUARY 3, 1905 |
| FEBRUARY 3, 1916 | to | JANUARY 22, 1917 |
| JANUARY 23, 1928 | to | FEBRUARY 9, 1929 |
| FEBRUARY 8, 1940 | to | JANUARY 26, 1941 |
| JANUARY 27, 1952 | to | FEBRUARY 13, 1953 |
| FEBRUARY 13, 1964 | to | FEBRUARY 1, 1965 |
| JANUARY 31, 1976 | to | FEBRUARY 17, 1977 |
| FEBRUARY 17, 1988 | to | FEBRUARY 5, 1989 |

## THE YEARS OF THE SNAKE

| | | |
|---|---|---|
| FEBRUARY 4, 1905 | *to* | JANUARY 24, 1906 |
| JANUARY 23, 1917 | *to* | FEBRUARY 10, 1918 |
| FEBRUARY 10, 1929 | *to* | JANUARY 29, 1930 |
| JANUARY 27, 1941 | *to* | FEBRUARY 14, 1942 |
| FEBRUARY 14, 1953 | *to* | FEBRUARY 2, 1954 |
| FEBRUARY 2, 1965 | *to* | JANUARY 20, 1966 |
| FEBRUARY 18, 1977 | *to* | FEBRUARY 6, 1978 |
| FEBRUARY 6, 1989 | *to* | JANUARY 26, 1990 |

## THE YEARS OF THE HORSE

| | | |
|---|---|---|
| JANUARY 25, 1906 | *to* | FEBRUARY 12, 1907 |
| FEBRUARY 11, 1918 | *to* | JANUARY 31, 1919 |
| JANUARY 30, 1930 | *to* | FEBRUARY 16, 1931 |
| FEBRUARY 15, 1942 | *to* | FEBRUARY 4, 1943 |
| FEBRUARY 3, 1954 | *to* | JANUARY 23, 1955 |
| JANUARY 21, 1966 | *to* | FEBRUARY 8, 1967 |
| FEBRUARY 7, 1978 | *to* | JANUARY 27, 1979 |
| JANUARY 27, 1990 | *to* | FEBRUARY 14, 1991 |

## THE YEARS OF THE GOAT

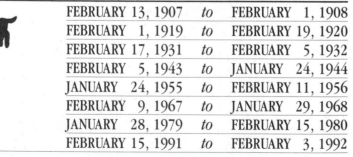

| | | |
|---|---|---|
| FEBRUARY 13, 1907 | *to* | FEBRUARY 1, 1908 |
| FEBRUARY 1, 1919 | *to* | FEBRUARY 19, 1920 |
| FEBRUARY 17, 1931 | *to* | FEBRUARY 5, 1932 |
| FEBRUARY 5, 1943 | *to* | JANUARY 24, 1944 |
| JANUARY 24, 1955 | *to* | FEBRUARY 11, 1956 |
| FEBRUARY 9, 1967 | *to* | JANUARY 29, 1968 |
| JANUARY 28, 1979 | *to* | FEBRUARY 15, 1980 |
| FEBRUARY 15, 1991 | *to* | FEBRUARY 3, 1992 |

# THE YEARS OF THE MONKEY

| | | |
|---|---|---|
| FEBRUARY 2, 1908 | *to* | JANUARY 21, 1909 |
| FEBRUARY 20, 1920 | *to* | FEBRUARY 7, 1921 |
| FEBRUARY 6, 1932 | *to* | JANUARY 25, 1933 |
| JANUARY 25, 1944 | *to* | FEBRUARY 12, 1945 |
| FEBRUARY 12, 1956 | *to* | JANUARY 30, 1957 |
| JANUARY 30, 1968 | *to* | FEBRUARY 16, 1969 |
| FEBRUARY 16, 1980 | *to* | FEBRUARY 4, 1981 |
| FEBRUARY 4, 1992 | *to* | JANUARY 22, 1993 |

# THE YEARS OF THE ROOSTER

| | | |
|---|---|---|
| JANUARY 22, 1909 | *to* | FEBRUARY 9, 1910 |
| FEBRUARY 8, 1921 | *to* | JANUARY 27, 1922 |
| JANUARY 26, 1933 | *to* | FEBRUARY 13, 1934 |
| FEBRUARY 13, 1945 | *to* | FEBRUARY 1, 1946 |
| JANUARY 31, 1957 | *to* | FEBRUARY 17, 1958 |
| FEBRUARY 17, 1969 | *to* | FEBRUARY 5, 1970 |
| FEBRUARY 5, 1981 | *to* | JANUARY 24, 1982 |
| JANUARY 23, 1993 | *to* | FEBRUARY 9, 1994 |

# THE YEARS OF THE DOG

| | | |
|---|---|---|
| FEBRUARY 10, 1910 | *to* | JANUARY 29, 1911 |
| JANUARY 28, 1922 | *to* | FEBRUARY 15, 1923 |
| FEBRUARY 14, 1934 | *to* | FEBRUARY 3, 1935 |
| FEBRUARY 2, 1946 | *to* | JANUARY 21, 1947 |
| FEBRUARY 18, 1958 | *to* | FEBRUARY 7, 1959 |
| FEBRUARY 6, 1970 | *to* | JANUARY 26, 1971 |
| JANUARY 25, 1982 | *to* | FEBRUARY 12, 1983 |
| FEBRUARY 10, 1994 | *to* | JANUARY 30, 1995 |

# THE BASIC ANIMAL PERSONALITIES

According to ancient Oriental beliefs, you have inherited many of the physical and emotional characteristics of the animal whose sign you were born under. For those of you born under signs such as the rat, pig, or dog, this may be upsetting news to you. After all, in our society pigs are regarded as fat, messy, selfish, lazy, and rude, while rats are regarded as being even worse than pigs! And who among us wants to be referred to as a dog? Don't be discouraged. To the Chinese these are three of the most desirable signs to be born under. Besides things could be worse: Buddha could have made us *all* asses!

Meanwhile, to paraphrase Popeye, "You is what you is," and now that you know what you "is," you'd better learn as much about your ancient roots as possible. To be forewarned is to be forearmed. Or, in your case, four-legged!

Once you accept your heritage and are comfortable with it, you will learn fascinating things about yourself. Indeed, personality traits which heretofore confused you will suddenly make sense. For example, if you just discovered that you are spiritually a pig, this new knowledge will explain why you have always felt a special empathy for policemen, and why you cry at barbecues. It also sheds light on why, when you go to football games, you root for the football.

Similarly, if you just discovered that you are a tiger, you now know why you craved Frosted Flakes as a child, and why you have always had a thing for guys named Tony. And certainly you snakes must be relieved to understand why, as an infant, you loved to play with rattles . . . or why you find yourself siding with laborers who are threatening to strike.

We know of one man who spent a fortune on psychiatric bills trying to understand why he felt trapped in both his career and his marriage. As it turned out, he was born under the sign of the rat, and his feelings were therefore quite normal. Once advised of this, his anxieties disappeared immediately.

Perhaps the fastest way to start developing a sense of your animal self is to learn about your basic animal personality.

# THE BASIC

# PIG

## PERSONALITY

Pigs are terrific people. They are trustworthy, loyal, hard-working, sincere, sociable, loving, intelligent, peaceable, sensitive and sensual. In fact, Will Rogers would have been closer to the mark if he had said, "I never met a *pig* I didn't like."

Pigs are also good providers: no matter how rough things become, they always bring home the bacon. Similarly, they are good with money and have an uncanny ability to turn virtually any container into a bank for coins. Some pigs are selfish and tend to hog things. Others are dull and uninteresting. Many are outright boars. But pigs have absolutely no control and frequently go hog-wild. Finally, pigs are incredibly sloppy... why do you think they are called pigs?

## PIGS AS PARENTS

From their children's point of view, pigs make wonderful parents—they never require them to clean up their messy rooms.

## FAMOUS PIGS

*Ronald Reagan*
*Woody Allen*
*Prince Rainier*
*Ernest Hemingway*
*Alfred Hitchcock*
*Maria Callas*
*Henry Kissinger*
*Lucille Ball*
*Rosalind Russell*
*Al Capone*

# WORDS OF CAUTION

☞ Be wary of real estate brokers who attempt to sell you houses made of wood or straw. Insist on brick, especially if you live in a geographical area where the wind huffs and puffs.

☞ Avoid people who make silk purses if they say you have beautiful ears.

☞ Protect your eyes at all times: pigs are prone to sties.

## THE BASIC

# RAT

## PERSONALITY

Rats are survivors. No matter how sticky the situation, they always manage to "squeak by." Rats aren't quitters either; even if a project is hopeless, they will stick with it to the bitter end, invariably being the last to abandon ship. But rats cannot be trusted: they are notorious for informing on their friends.

Rats love the hectic pace of the business world and—given their propensity for rat races—make very good corporate men and women. However, they seldom rise above middle-management positions to become the "Big Cheese."

## RATS AS PARENTS

Rats make dedicated parents. This is due to the guilt they have from bearing children with buck teeth— a genetic trait they can't help but nonetheless punish themselves for.

## FAMOUS RATS

*William
   Shakespeare
Charlotte Brontë
Wolfgang Amadeus
   Mozart
Jimmy Carter
Sidney Poitier
Maurice Chevalier
Prince Charles
Adlai Stevenson
Doris Day
Marlon Brando*

## WORDS OF CAUTION

☞ Refuse invitations to cheese tasting parties (as these are clearly traps).

☞ Avoid research labs.

☞ Watch out for FBI agents who will try to get you to "rat" on your friends.

DON'T GIVE UP THE SHIP!

## THE BASIC

# BULL

### PERSONALITY

Never take anything a bull tells you at face value, for it is well known that bulls exaggerate terribly and often lie outright. They frequently get away with it because they bully people into believing their outrageous stories.

Bulls are boisterous, easily annoyed, and hard to calm down. If you get on their back, they kick up a storm. But if you get on their good side and don't give them any reason to beef, bulls can be led as though they had a ring in their nose.

Bulls also have good financial judgment and are a good source of stock market tips, but always check their facts—otherwise you might wind up with a bum steer.

## BULLS AS PARENTS

Bulls make okay parents, as long as the other parent is not born under the sign of the dog. This union produces short, squat children that look like their namesakes: bulldogs.

## FAMOUS BULLS

*Dustin Hoffman*
*Walt Disney*
*Gerald Ford*
*Margaret Thatcher*
*Vanessa Redgrave*
*Peter Sellers*
*Vincent Van Gogh*
*Sammy Davis, Jr.*
*Robert Redford*
*Charlie Chaplin*

## WORDS OF CAUTION

☞ Avoid going to Spain! While the consequences are far less great, stay away from shops that sell china.

☞ Never fall asleep at a McDonald's or a Burger King, especially if your name is Patty.

☞ Avoid saying socially embarrassing things—it could lead to a fatal case of hoof in mouth disease.

## THE BASIC

# TIGER

## PERSONALITY

Tigers are a wild bunch. They love to party and are always out stalking a good time. Not surprisingly, tigers would have been very happy in the "Roaring Twenties."

Despite their ferocious appearance, tigers are really just big pussycats. They tend to be very insecure and love to be held. (Most people think "Hold That Tiger" is a football cheer. Actually, it's a love song!)

Tigers hate to work and frequently complain that "it's a jungle out there." The last thing they want to do is grab the world by the tail—they would much rather play than work. In fact, to them life is one big circus, and they are the center ring attraction.

## TIGERS AS PARENTS

Tiger parents are strict disciplinarians and often resort to using whips and chairs as aids in training their children.

## FAMOUS TIGERS

*Ho Chi Minh*
*Ludwig van*
  *Beethoven*
*Queen Elizabeth II*
*Emily Brontë*
*Marilyn Monroe*
*Alec Guinness*
*Dwight Eisenhower*
*Groucho Marx*
*Charles De Gaulle*
*Rudolf Nureyev*

## WORDS OF CAUTION

☞ Stay away from guys named Ringling, Barnum, or Bailey.

☞ Avoid the Super Bowl and the World Series. Anything to do with "big game" is dangerous for you.

☞ Be sure not to fall into your car's gas tank when filling up with Exxon.

# THE BASIC

# CAT

## PERSONALITY

Cats go out of their way to look for trouble; after all, they believe they have nine lives to live. Fortunately, they always land on their feet, no matter now harrowing the experience.

Cats are finicky. They are notoriously fussy eaters and will often skip meals in favor of a glass of milk. They are fastidious dressers and are always preening. Despite this, cats have an irrational attraction to litter.

Cats are quiet and prefer body language to verbal expression: When they're upset they arch their backs defiantly; when they're contented, they purr.

## CATS AS PARENTS

Cats, like pigs, make ideal parents—as far as their children are concerned—since they love litter and don't impose many household chores.

## FAMOUS CATS

*Dr. Benjamin Spock*
*Peter Falk*
*Albert Einstein*
*Queen Victoria*
*David Frost*
*Fidel Castro*
*Ingrid Bergman*
*Henry Miller*
*Ali McGraw*
*Joseph Stalin*

## WORDS OF CAUTION

☞ Be sure to lock your house at night—otherwise a cat burglar might get you.

☞ Avoid tennis racquet and violin string companies!

☞ Stay off hot tin roofs.

# THE BASIC

# DRAGON

## PERSONALITY

**D**ragons are romantics. Females are into Gothic novels, while males fancy themselves brave saviors, ready to rescue damsels in distress.

But, in fact, dragons are not brave at all. They have such a strong aversion to (k)nights that they rarely go out after dark. They never take risks because they are afraid they will get into trouble and be sent to jail— and they *hate* the very thought of dungeons.

Dragons tend to be clumsy and slow, and are painfully shy. Accordingly, they lack social graces and tend to be real flamers.

## DRAGONS AS PARENTS

Dragons make good parents, insofar as they are understanding, but their lack of energy means that dragon offspring better rely on someone other than Dad to teach them how to play baseball, ride a bike, and fly a kite.

## FAMOUS DRAGONS

*Ringo Starr*
*Salvador Dali*
*Kirk Douglas*
*Anthony Quinn*
*Joan of Arc*
*Jimmy Connors*
*John Lennon*
*Betty Grable*
*Frank Sinatra*
*John Paul Getty*

# WORDS OF CAUTION

☞ Avoid men with the title "Sir," especially if their name is Lancelot or George.

☞ Don't take piano lessons—dragons have trouble with scales.

☞ Be careful not to breathe out too heavily in areas where there are gasoline or other flammable fumes.

# THE BASIC

# SNAKE

## PERSONALITY

Snakes have a problem with self esteem. This stems from biblical times when their ancestor caused that scandal in Eden. As a result, many snakes carry terrible guilt with them today, and it is not surprising that many are spineless low-life types. But this belies the true snake personality. Snakes have a lot of class and are extremely charming.

Snakes are intellectual and like to "wrap their minds around things." They make excellent students as well as diligent workers, since they love to sink their fangs into a project. But management should be advised to treat snake employees well—they won't hesitate to strike if they feel their rights are tread upon.

## SNAKES AS PARENTS

Snakes make indulgent parents, but snake offspring must look elsewhere for moral role models. Their parents don't have much in the way of backbone.

## FAMOUS SNAKES

*Howard Hughes*
*Greta Garbo*
*Princess Grace*
*Abraham Lincoln*
*Henry Ford II*
*Ann-Margret*
*Carole King*
*Johannes Brahms*
*Indira Gandhi*
*Jacqueline Onassis*

## WORDS OF CAUTION

 Be careful when mowing the lawn, another snake in the grass could be hiding there.

 Avoid factories that make fancy belts, handbags, or shoes.

 Watch out for men with flutes and straw baskets.

PLATO

INDIA

A CHARMING GUIDE

INDIA

## THE BASIC

# HORSE

## PERSONALITY

Horses are people of extremes: either they are hard workers who plod steadily through life, or high-spirited risk takers who hate to be saddled with responsibility; either they are thoroughbred blue bloods, or half breeds of dubious, sometimes even wild descent; either they are super achievers who reach the winner's circle at an early age, or losers who are always on the wrong track; either they are loyal team players who pull together, or loners who are always trying to jockey for position for the big win. But no matter what extreme a horse is, chances are he or she has a stable of good friends.

## HORSES AS PARENTS

Children of horse parents can count on a hearty breakfast of hot oats and sugar and at bedtime, a warm, cozy blanket.

## FAMOUS HORSES

*Theodore Roosevelt*
*Neil Armstrong*
*Paul McCartney*
*Raquel Welch*
*Pearl Bailey*
*Rembrandt*
*Ulysses S. Grant*
*Franklin Delano*
   *Roosevelt*
*Billy Graham*
*Anwar Sadat*

## WORDS OF CAUTION

☞ Be careful who you horse around with—you could be branded for life.

☞ Avoid glue factories and dog food plants.

☞ Don't drink the water in foreign countries. You could come down with the "trots."

## THE BASIC

# GOAT

## PERSONALITY

Goats are ornery. They are stubborn and gruff and have an annoying habit of butting in on everybody's business. However, they themselves are secretive and will never give you any inside information, no matter how hard you milk them. This combination of traits makes goats difficult to live with. But given a chance, goats will prove themselves unselfish, loyal, and extremely loving.

Goats are very competitive. To them, life is one big game of "King of the Mountain," and they will do anything to get to the top. Once there, a goat's sure-footedness will make it hard to topple him.

## GOATS AS PARENTS

Goats make wonderful parents. After all, they invented "kids"!

## FAMOUS GOATS

*Andy Warhol*
*Barbara Walters*
*James Michener*
*Sir Laurence Olivier*
*Pierre Elliott Trudeau*
*Thomas Edison*
*Catherine Deneuve*
*Muhammad Ali*
*Mark Twain*
*Alexander Graham Bell*

## WORDS OF CAUTION

 Lie about your age—no one likes an old goat.

 Be sure to defend yourself—don't be a scapegoat.

 Rubbish!

# THE BASIC
# MONKEY
## PERSONALITY

Monkeys are very silly. They are constantly chattering, will do anything for a laugh, and have the attention span of a two-year-old. Monkeys are great practical jokers. Indeed, they are a barrel of laughs and love to perform.

Monkeys are climbers: social climbers as well as climbers up the corporate ladder. Unfortunately, they're also swingers, and are not adverse to a little monkeying around—even if it means losing all they have worked so hard to achieve.

Monkeys cannot be depended on; they will just as soon leave you up a tree as look at you. On the other hand, they themselves can be *very* dependent on others, and once you get one on your back, he's pretty tough to shake.

## MONKEYS AS PARENTS

Monkey parents have a great responsibility, for whatever their children see them do, they are sure to imitate.

## FAMOUS MONKEYS

*Walter Matthau*
*Milton Berle*
*Charles Dickens*
*Nelson Rockefeller*
*Lyndon B. Johnson*
*Edward Kennedy*
*Mick Jagger*
*Joan Crawford*
*Bette Davis*
*Federico Fellini*

## WORDS OF CAUTION

☞ Hear no evil.

☞ See no evil.

☞ Speak no evil.

## THE BASIC

# ROOSTER

## PERSONALITY

Roosters are very cocky, often without good reason. For example, despite the fact that they are up and on the job at the crack of dawn, many rooster men can barely scratch out a living. As a result, they are often henpecked at home and have to compensate for their lack of male accomplishment in other ways, such as wearing brightly colored clothes and strutting around in a self-important manner. Because they are often low on the corporate pecking order, many roosters achieve a sense of self-worth only by surrounding themselves with subservient types who won't challenge their authority—in other words, chickens.

Roosters hate responsibility. The males fancy themselves as studs, but when it comes to helping raise the kids, they often flee the coop.

## ROOSTERS AS PARENTS

Pity the children who have roosters for parents, for they will never be allowed to sleep past dawn.

## FAMOUS ROOSTERS

*Elton John*
*Pope Paul VI*
*Elia Kazan*
*Katharine*
   *Hepburn*
*Grover Cleveland*
*Andrei Gromyko*
*William Faulkner*
*Alex Haley*
*Peter Ustinov*
*Yves Montand*

## WORDS OF CAUTION

☞ Avoid Frank Perdue and Colonel Sanders.

☞ Don't worry if people ignore your cockamamie ideas.

☞ Never marry anyone born under another sign. Otherwise, your children will be half-cocked.

# THE BASIC

# DOG

## PERSONALITY

Dogs are warm, loyal, loving, and make wonderful best friends. They are good judges of character and can invariably sniff out the truth.

Dogs are intelligent. They are easily trained, eager to learn, and require little more than a kind word as a reward. However, many dogs have low self-esteem and humble themselves by doing menial chores (such as bringing their spouse the newspaper and slippers) in order to be liked. In some cases this self-esteem problem is so bad that they actually cannot hold down a job and have to go from table to table, begging for scraps of food.

Some dogs are high-strung and are always ready to pick a bone with you, but in most cases their bark is worse than their bite.

## DOGS AS PARENTS

Dogs make good parents, but they expect their children to be obedient and well-groomed at all times. Dog parents understand puppy love.

## FAMOUS DOGS

*Ralph Nader*
*Churchill*
*Charles Bronson*
*Zsa Zsa Gabor*
*Sophia Loren*
*Cher*
*Liza Minnelli*
*Golda Meir*
*Carol Burnett*
*Elvis Presley*

## WORDS OF CAUTION

☞ Curb your desire to chase cars and attack mailmen so that you don't hurt or embarrass yourself.

☞ Be careful where you hide your valuables— you might forget where you buried them.

☞ Avoid flea markets.

# ANIMAL CAREERS

It's been said that one man's junk is another's treasure. That's sort of the way it works in Chinese astrology, too: one animal's bad luck can turn out to be another's big chance. The secret comes in knowing how to recognize opportunity when it knocks, and that requires more insight into your animal horoscope.

## AS A PIG

Pigs are better suited to some professions than to others. For example, they are natural hams and are virtually assured of success in an acting career. Similarly, their natural porcine instincts indicate that they would excel as ham radio operators or as mud wrestlers.

**RECOMMENDED CAREERS** include anything requiring patience and understanding, such as: teacher, philosopher, clergyman, psychiatrist, guidance counselor, poet, nurse, doctor.

**CAREERS TO AVOID** include anything requiring you to be tough, hard-nosed, and aggressive, such as: politician, lawyer, coach, negotiator, salesman.

# AS A RAT

Rats are opportunists—they do well by lurking in the background and waiting for the right moment before making their move. Deceit and underhandedness are their long suits. They make out well as industrial spies, since ratting on fellow employees is no problem.

**RECOMMENDED CAREERS** include anything requiring craftiness and strategy, such as: military leader, gambler, con artist, football quarterback, film director, politician, salesman.

**CAREERS TO AVOID** include anything requiring you to follow orders, such as: civil servant, assembly line worker, secretary, janitor, enlisted military man/woman.

# AS A BULL

Bulls would do well to pursue any career which requires a fast talker. Areas such as politics, sales, and advertising are perfect opportunities for people who are full of bull.

**RECOMMENDED CAREERS** include anything requiring loyalty, dedication, and attention to detail, such as: bureaucrat, civil servant, fund raiser, professional athlete, coach, political appointee.

**CAREERS TO AVOID** include anything requiring creative expression and interpretation, such as: advertising writer, entertainer, novelist, artist, dancer.

# AS A TIGER

Tigers are authority figures and command a lot of respect. They make excellent television pitchmen, especially for breakfast cereals and gasoline. Tigers also do well as doormen, rugby players, military officers—or as anything that requires wearing stripes.

**RECOMMENDED CAREERS** include anything requiring strength and physical perserverance, such as: wrestler, boxer, skier, marathon racer, soldier of fortune, bouncer, construction worker.

**CAREERS TO AVOID** include anything requiring patience and long attention spans, such as: air traffic controller, clergyman, surgeon, marriage counselor, psychiatrist.

# AS A CAT

Cats are well advised to sit and wait until the right job opportunity comes along for them to pounce on. However, they do well in careers requiring subtle, quiet movements—or in anything that involves climbing trees.

**RECOMMENDED CAREERS** include anything requiring an outgoing personality, such as: entertainer, politician, social butterfly, talk show host, gossip columnist, public relations agent.

**CAREERS TO AVOID** include anything requiring confrontation, such as: soldier, lawyer/judge, policeman/woman, negotiator, teacher.

## AS A DRAGON

There aren't too many opportunities which take advantage of a dragon's innate skills, except maybe flame swallowing. The only dragon who has made it big in modern times is the Loch Ness monster, and the chances of his letting anyone else in on his scam are slight.

**RECOMMENDED CAREERS** include anything requiring a strong, domineering personality, such as: labor leader, politician, chairman of the board, pro football player, military leader, school headmaster.

**CAREERS TO AVOID** include anything requiring following orders, such as: ship's crew member, bureaucratic staff member, municipal worker, waiter/waitress, flight attendant.

## AS A SNAKE

Snakes' best bet to make a lot of money fast is through playing craps, inasmuch as their ability to roll "snake eyes" is uncanny. They might consider selling fancy clothes, with boas as a specialty, if they don't find the field too constricting.

**RECOMMENDED CAREERS** include anything requiring thoughtful analysis, such as: professor, research scientist, engineer, philosopher, historian, investment analyst, judge.

**CAREERS TO AVOID** include anything requiring you to think on your feet, such as: salesman, politician, spy, Presidential press spokesperson, sports commentator.

## AS A HORSE

Since horses are at home on the range, they make excellent chefs. Of course some horses have been known to do well as entrepreneurs, given their ability to buck the system.

**RECOMMENDED CAREERS** include anything requiring you to work essentially alone, such as: private detective, cabinet maker, artist, novelist, illustrator, sculptor, forest ranger.

**CAREERS TO AVOID** include anything requiring a team effort, such as: professional basketball, baseball, football or hockey player, assembly line worker, filmmaker, nurse, doctor, construction worker.

## AS A GOAT

The innate stubbornness of goats makes them perfectly suited for careers in law and labor negotiating, and their inherent nimble-footedness enables them to excel as mountaineering guides or disco dancers.

**RECOMMENDED CAREERS** include anything requiring a constant change of pace, such as: actor, traveling salesman/woman, film director, soldier, travel guide, editor.

**CAREERS TO AVOID** include anything involving a set routine, such as: mailman, bus driver, conductor, assembly line worker.

# AS A MONKEY

Monkeys do best in all areas of monkey business. They also excel as plumbers, mechanics, or anything requiring the use of a monkey wrench. If religiously inclined, they could consider becoming a monk.

**RECOMMENDED CAREERS** include anything requiring cunning and "one-upsmanship," such as: Hollywood producer, oil magnate wheeler-dealer, talent agent, public relations agent, CIA agent.

**CAREERS TO AVOID** include anything that has a regular course of procedure, such as: waiter/waitress, bus driver, flight attendant, store clerk, shoe salesman, toll collector, truck driver.

# AS A ROOSTER

Roosters do well as public relations agents—they are always crowing about something—or as operators in charge of wake-up calls. They might also do well as bartenders who specialize in mixing fancy cocktails.

**RECOMMENDED CAREERS** include anything requiring pomp and circumstance, such as: military officer, government official, actor, orchestra conductor, stripper.

**CAREERS TO AVOID** include anything requiring humility and modesty, such as: monk, nun, social worker, missionary.

# AS A DOG

Dogs make excellent detectives, wine masters, perfume makers, or anything requiring a keen sense of smell. They also make successful consumer watchdogs.

**RECOMMENDED CAREERS** include anything requiring creative rather than business ability, such as: writer, artist, dancer, craftsman, poet, teacher, film director, designer. **CAREERS TO AVOID** include anything requiring traditional business acumen, such as: banker, financial analyst, marketing director, real estate broker, film producer.

# ANIMAL COMPATIBILITY

Of all the implications of your animal horoscope, your compatibility chart has more influence over your future happiness than any other single element. It can help you determine whom you should marry, who would make a good business partner or boss, who would be a best friend. Everybody has two animal types with whom he is compatible and three with whom he is not.

| If you are a: | You are compatible with: | You are not compatible with: |
|---|---|---|
| **PIG** | Goats and Cats | Snakes, Bulls, and Roosters |
| **RAT** | Monkeys and Dragons | Dogs, Horses, and Tigers |
| **BULL** | Roosters and Snakes | Pigs, Cats, and Goats |
| **TIGER** | Dogs and Horses | Rats, Monkeys, and Dragons |
| **CAT** | Pigs and Goats | Roosters, Bulls, and Snakes |
| **DRAGON** | Rats and Monkeys | Dogs, Horses, and Tigers |

| If you are a: | You are compatible with: | You are not compatible with: |
|---|---|---|
| **SNAKE** | Bulls and Roosters | Pigs, Goats, and Cats |
| **HORSE** | Tigers and Dogs | Rats, Monkeys, and Dragons |
| **GOAT** | Cats and Pigs | Snakes, Roosters, and Bulls |
| **MONKEY** | Dragons and Rats | Dogs, Tigers, and Horses |
| **ROOSTER** | Snakes and Bulls | Cats, Pigs, and Goats |
| **DOG** | Horses and Tigers | Dragons, Rats, and Monkeys |

# ANIMAL SEXUALITY

The better you know yourself, the easier it will be for you to capitalize on your own inherent personality traits to help you get what you want in life. Like members of the opposite sex.

The first step toward that end is seeing yourself as others see you, and that's one of the things you will learn in this chapter.

Perhaps even more important than self-enlightenment is the knowledge Buddha imparts by pointing out what stirs the animal instinct in others.

|  | *MALE* | *FEMALE* |
|---|---|---|
| **PIGS** | Male pigs are not chauvinists. On the contrary, they are warm, loving and respectful. Because they are essentially loyal, male pigs are faithful lovers. Not surprisingly, the way to a male pig's heart is through his stomach. | Female pigs can be very sexy and socially outgoing. However, they are extremely gullible and will believe just about any hogwash they are told. They have delusions of social grandeur (who, Moi?), but once married, they make excellent mates and indulgent lovers. |
| **RATS** | Male rats are deceitful, dishonest, scheming, and underhanded. It is not by accident that feminists say "men are rats"! | Female rats are, for the most part, quiet, shy, and unattractive. In fact, they are downright "mousey." However, every so often you will find a nice little tail. |

|  | *MALE* | *FEMALE* |
|---|---|---|
| **BULLS** | Male bulls make incredibly strong lovers. In fact, they are real studs. However, they are totally without sensitivity and have no use for foreplay. They are easily aroused, especially if their partner wears red lingerie. | Female bulls aren't at all into sex. Although some of them have amazing figures (udderly incredible!), most of them are real cows. |
| **TIGERS** | There's nothing timid about these guys—they are *real* tigers in the bedroom. Give a male tiger half a chance and he'll have his paws all over you. | Female tigers are just as bad (good?). They tend to be very kinky, and many of them are into discipline, with whips and chairs their preferred props. |
| **CATS** | Male cats are notorious as lovers. They just can't seem to get enough sex, and even if they have an indulgent mate, they will still stray. | Female cats tend to be a little standoffish at first, but if you treat them right, you will have them purring in no time. |
| **DRAGONS** | Are you kidding? | Are you kidding? |
| **SNAKES** | Male snakes tend to be real outdoor types and love doing it in the grass. They are real charmers. | Female snakes are a bit less adventurous and like nothing more than a good old fashioned tight hug. They are also real charmers. |
| **HORSES** | Male horses are definitely studs. They will very likely invite you up to see their etchings or other horse-drawn items. They love to sow their wild oats, and while they may pledge you their love, we wouldn't place any bets on it. | Female horses will do everything in their power to lead you down the bridal path. Once married, though, they make terrible nags. |

|  | *MALE* | *FEMALE* |
|---|---|---|
| **GOATS** | Beware of the male goat! This horny creature has one thing on his mind: sex. Male goats are very physical and will contrive any excuse they can think of to touch you. If brushed off they will reply, "Oh, I was just kidding around!" | Female goats are notoriously stubborn; they will keep after a man until they get him. They are especially attracted to men with goatees and like to be taken out to eat. Although female goats are not very pretty, they often have nice cans. |
| **MONKEYS** | Male monkeys are selfish lovers. They care only about immediate gratification and don't understand the meaning of the word loyalty. However, if you are looking for an extramarital affair, you can't beat one of these guys: they are experts at monkey business. | Female monkeys are insanely jealous lovers, ever since King Kong lost his heart to Fay Wray. They need loads of attention and reassurance or they are likely to go ape. |
| **ROOSTERS** | Rooster men think they are Buddha's gift to women. They regard themselves as sex symbols and think that women are waiting around to be noticed by them. As a result, they have enormous egos and are extremely cocky. | Females of the species pale by comparison to their colorful male counterparts. They have conservative views toward sex and won't try anything new because they are too chicken. |
| **DOGS** | Male dogs are loyal, obedient lovers. They are romantic and love to go for long walks. Easily hurt, male dogs often beg for affection. Once married they make easy-going spouses; if a bone of contention arises, they would just as soon bury it. | Female dogs are very sexy. When they walk they wiggle their tails in a very fetching way. They are adventurous lovers, always willing to learn new tricks. They don't even mind being tied up if it pleases their "master." |

# OFFICIAL ANIMAL SPOTTER'S GUIDE

Now that you know which animals to go after and which ones to avoid, you have to know how to spot the various animal types so that you will know where to focus your efforts.

This is actually a lot easier than it sounds, since according to the tenets of animal horoscope, people born under the sign of a specific animal have many of the same physical—as well as personality—traits as the "host" animal.

Although love can strike anytime, anyplace, this Official Animal Spotter's Guide has been keyed to the type of environment in which it is most likely to be used—a cocktail party or a singles bar.

## *OFFICIAL ANIMAL SPOTTER'S GUIDE*

# PIGS

Pigs can be identified by their fat bodies, pink complexions, and broad, turned-up noses. Pig women often wear their hair in two small braids, or "tails."

In social situations, pigs are the ones who station themselves near the food and don't move. They make good audiences and will respond to even the stupidest joke with squeals of delight and laughter.

If you see someone attempting to uncork a wine bottle with his tail, you know it's a pig.

### PICK-UP LINES TO USE ON PIGS

66Wanna eat?99

66You have such a cute nose!99

66This is the wurst party I've ever seen.99

## *OFFICIAL ANIMAL SPOTTER'S GUIDE*

# RATS

Rats are distinguished by their small hands and feet. Invariably, you will find them at the bar, next to the cheese.

The males often wear their hair slicked back and frequently sport whiskers. The females like to wear their hair teased or "ratted" in the manner of fifties rock-and-roll singers. Both sexes are likely to be wearing business attire, since they love the rat race of corporate life.

If you are looking for a rat (monkeys and dragons take notice!), don't go to a fancy club: rats prefer small "holes in the wall." Try a little sweet talk and flattery and you will find that your rat is easily trapped.

### PICK-UP LINES TO USE ON RATS

66How do you manage to stay so sleek?99

66You'll love my place . . . it's a basement apartment.99

66So you're a golfer, eh? I'll bet you never get caught in a sand trap.99

## *OFFICIAL ANIMAL SPOTTER'S GUIDE*

# BULL

Bulls were the first "punk" animals and can be identified by the trendy rings they wear through their noses. Bulls love to dance, or "go hoofing" as they call it. If you want a bull to make a pass at you, wear something red.

Bulls are great conversationalists and can talk for hours, but you should never believe a word they say.

Some bulls can't hold their liquor and fall asleep after one drink. These are called "bull dozers" and aren't much fun. Some bull women are unattractive. They are called "bull dogs" and should be avoided. Some bulls are from France. They are called "bull frogs" and are very charming.

### PICK-UP LINES TO USE ON BULLS

❝Actually, I do very well . . . I'm a lawnmower salesman for Toro.❞

❝Of course I believe you. Why do you ask?❞

❝I'll love you 'till the cows come home.❞

## *OFFICIAL ANIMAL SPOTTER'S GUIDE*

# TIGERS

Tigers have a thing for stripes, so be on the lookout for military men, ex-cons, rugby players, and guys wearing rep ties. Tigers often start singing old Princeton songs after they have had a few drinks, even if they never went to college.

Tiger women are particularly dangerous; once they get their claws into you, it's all over.

### PICK-UP LINES TO USE ON TIGERS

66You look great in stripes.99

66You're so poised. Early training, I suppose?99

66I'd love to grab you by the tail.99

## *OFFICIAL ANIMAL SPOTTER'S GUIDE*

# CATS

Cats are "night people"; they enjoy a howling good time and think nothing of staying out all night. If you see a lot of Jaguars parked in front of a bar, chances are there arc a lot of cats inside.

Cat women are easy to spot: they always order drinks made with cream. They tend to be real sex kittens and won't hesitate to climb onto your lap.

Male cats think of themselves as being very cool. They are frequently named Tom or Morris. Although they are not big drinkers, they do like a little nip from time to time.

### PICK-UP LINES TO USE ON CATS

**❝**I feel I met you in a previous life.**❞**

**❝**Would you like some chocolate mouse? I mean, mousse?**❞**

**❝**What lovely nails you have!**❞**

*OFFICIAL ANIMAL SPOTTER'S GUIDE*

# DRAGONS

**D**ragons have incredibly strong breath. Most are big-boned and have large features. As a rule they have horrible greenish complexions.

Dragons are totally lacking in social graces and tend to be real flamers. They have awful senses of humor and tell terrible jokes, which they usually follow with ''Doesn't that slay you?''

## PICK-UP LINES TO USE ON DRAGONS

66Actually, green is my favorite color. . .99

66When you breathe in my ear I get so hot!99

66I'm a simple man . . . my home is hardly what you'd call a castle.99

## *OFFICIAL ANIMAL SPOTTER'S GUIDE*

# SNAKES

Snakes are real charmers. They will worm their way into your heart, and then sink their fangs into you. The males can be identified by their belts and fancy boots. Females love to wear boas and slink across the room.

Snakes of both sexes are spineless and will resort to bribes to win your favor. Don't be tempted to accept "free" gifts of apples or "magic" oil.

Although snakes are easy to identify in bars, they're hard to spot in the grass.

## PICK-UP LINES TO USE ON SNAKES

**❝**Gosh, you sure have some slinky moves on the dance floor!**❞**

**❝**You have winning eyes.**❞**

**❝**So you're a gardener, eh? I love plants myself.**❞**

## *OFFICIAL ANIMAL SPOTTER'S GUIDE*

# HORSES

Horse women can be readily identified by their pony tails and their big, ungainly smiles. They're a little on the kinky side, and love whips and boots. They wear large, clunky shoes and favor saddle bags instead of purses.

Horse men are real studs, and they act like it. They will very likely invite you up to see their etchings or other horse-drawn items. Horse men love to sow their wild oats, and even though they may pledge you their love, we wouldn't place any bets on it.

Horses are very racy, and the wilder ones often travel in packs.

## PICK-UP LINES TO USE ON HORSES

**"Hi, Sugar..."**

**"I like a woman (man) with horse sense."**

**"I'd like to stirrup a little excitement with you."**

## *OFFICIAL ANIMAL SPOTTER'S GUIDE*

# GOATS

**G**oats stand out in a crowd; they are the ones who order a six-pack and eat the cans instead of drinking the beer. If you are trying to have a conversation and someone keeps butting in, chances are it's a goat.

Goats of both sexes are frequently horny, so if you play your cards right, it should be easy to get your goat.

Because they are sure-footed, goats make excellent dancers.

### PICK-UP LINES TO USE ON GOATS

**66**You're so gruff . . . I like that in a man (woman).**99**

**66**I don't think you're stubborn . . . I think you just have a lot of integrity.**99**

**66**Love your beard . . . :**99**

## *OFFICIAL ANIMAL SPOTTER'S GUIDE*

# MONKEYS

The monkey is the one drinking the banana daiquiri. Monkeys love to chatter away all night and do imitations of people. They are a barrel of laughs.

If you spot a monkey woman and want to pick her up, make sure that she is unescorted—the guy she may be with could be a real gorilla.

A word of caution: some male monkeys wear eye shadow and have no interest in women. These are "chimp pansies" and should be avoided...unless you're into that sort of thing.

## PICK-UP LINES TO USE ON MONKEYS

66So, I hear you're a real swinger.99

66Wow... you're a regular barrel of laughs!99

66This place is a zoo... let's split.99

## *OFFICIAL ANIMAL SPOTTER'S GUIDE*

# ROOSTERS

Roosters are easily recognized because they are always crowing about something.

The males are very macho and tend to strut rather than walk. Many flaunt colorful combs in the fashion of Edd "Kookie" Byrnes from the old *77 Sunset Strip* TV series.

If you want to make it with a rooster, get an early start . . . they can't stay out late because they have to get up at the crack of dawn.

## PICK-UP LINES TO USE ON ROOSTERS

**"**Like I always say, 'early to bed, early to rise.'**"**

**"**I like you . . . you're a bit cocky, but I like it.**"**

**"**Come on, Baby. . . don't be chicken.**"**

## *OFFICIAL ANIMAL SPOTTER'S GUIDE*

# DOGS

**D**ogs of both sexes are well-heeled and love to wear expensive clothes, especially shiny coats. They absolutely love to flaunt jewelry: the women often wear expensive chokers, while the men love to show off their dog tags.

Dogs are easy to pick up since they're always anxious to go out. They become infatuated easily, but nine out of ten times it's only puppy love.

### PICK-UP LINES TO USE ON DOGS

**66**So . . . wanna go out?**99**

**66**My ears perked up the minute I heard your name.**99**

**66**Hey, baby, . . . what makes you tick?**99**

# CO-SIGNS:
# WHEN EAST MEETS
# WEST

In the introduction to this book we recalled the sixties, when people related strongly to their western zodiac signs. Now you have opened your eyes to Oriental astrology, and that's good. But you can't ignore the western sign under which you were born either, for an understanding of both birth signs is essential to knowing yourself.

This is particularly true since Oriental astrology deals with instinctive, rather than rational behavior, and failure to anticipate this aspect of your personality could lead to disaster. The following wheels show at a glance what to expect when the two signs combine.

# THE PIG

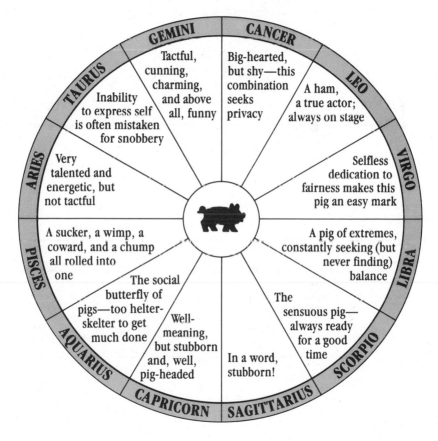

GEMINI — Tactful, cunning, charming, and above all, funny

CANCER — Big-hearted, but shy—this combination seeks privacy

TAURUS — Inability to express self is often mistaken for snobbery

LEO — A ham, a true actor; always on stage

ARIES — Very talented and energetic, but not tactful

VIRGO — Selfless dedication to fairness makes this pig an easy mark

PISCES — A sucker, a wimp, a coward, and a chump all rolled into one

LIBRA — A pig of extremes, constantly seeking (but never finding) balance

AQUARIUS — The social butterfly of pigs—too helter-skelter to get much done

SCORPIO — The sensuous pig—always ready for a good time

CAPRICORN — Well-meaning, but stubborn and, well, pig-headed

SAGITTARIUS — In a word, stubborn!

# THE RAT

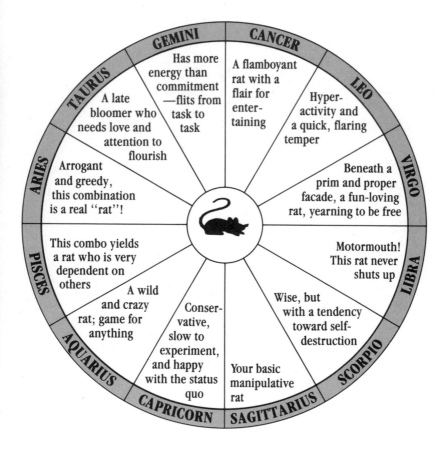

**GEMINI** — Has more energy than commitment —flits from task to task

**CANCER** — A flamboyant rat with a flair for entertaining

**TAURUS** — A late bloomer who needs love and attention to flourish

**LEO** — Hyperactivity and a quick, flaring temper

**ARIES** — Arrogant and greedy, this combination is a real "rat"!

**VIRGO** — Beneath a prim and proper facade, a fun-loving rat, yearning to be free

**PISCES** — This combo yields a rat who is very dependent on others

**LIBRA** — Motormouth! This rat never shuts up

**AQUARIUS** — A wild and crazy rat; game for anything

**CAPRICORN** — Conservative, slow to experiment, and happy with the status quo

**SCORPIO** — Wise, but with a tendency toward self-destruction

**SAGITTARIUS** — Your basic manipulative rat

# THE BULL

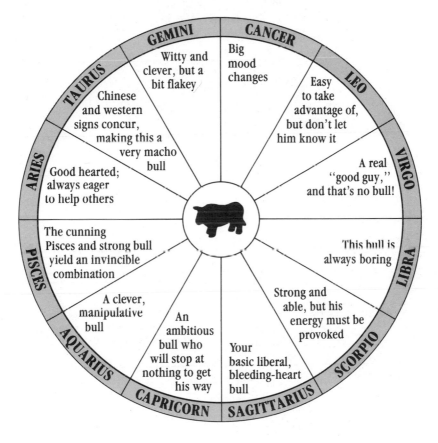

**GEMINI**
Witty and clever, but a bit flakey

**CANCER**
Big mood changes

**TAURUS**
Chinese and western signs concur, making this a very macho bull

**LEO**
Easy to take advantage of, but don't let him know it

**ARIES**
Good hearted; always eager to help others

**VIRGO**
A real "good guy," and that's no bull!

**PISCES**
The cunning Pisces and strong bull yield an invincible combination

**LIBRA**
This bull is always boring

A clever, manipulative bull

**SCORPIO**
Strong and able, but his energy must be provoked

**AQUARIUS**

**CAPRICORN**
An ambitious bull who will stop at nothing to get his way

**SAGITTARIUS**
Your basic liberal, bleeding-heart bull

# THE TIGER

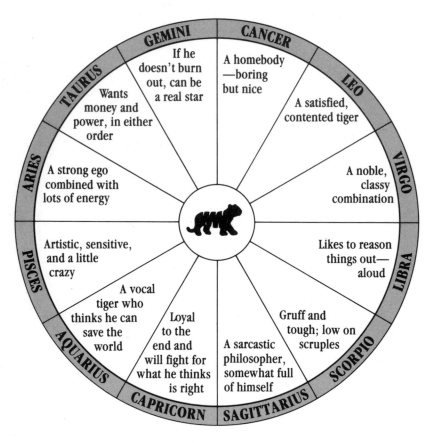

**GEMINI:** If he doesn't burn out, can be a real star

**CANCER:** A homebody —boring but nice

**TAURUS:** Wants money and power, in either order

**LEO:** A satisfied, contented tiger

**ARIES:** A strong ego combined with lots of energy

**VIRGO:** A noble, classy combination

**PISCES:** Artistic, sensitive, and a little crazy

**LIBRA:** Likes to reason things out— aloud

**AQUARIUS:** A vocal tiger who thinks he can save the world

**CAPRICORN:** Loyal to the end and will fight for what he thinks is right

**SAGITTARIUS:** A sarcastic philosopher, somewhat full of himself

**SCORPIO:** Gruff and tough; low on scruples

# THE CAT

**GEMINI** — This is the fun-loving cat

**CANCER** — A deep thinker—more mature than other cats

**TAURUS** — Would rather curl in front of the fire than go out and have fun

**LEO** — Looks and acts like a leader, but in reality may not be able to cut it

**ARIES** — Energetic; always looking for a challenge

**VIRGO** — A worry wart who never relaxes

**PISCES** — Needs lots of love, yet isn't loving unless coaxed

**LIBRA** — Quick with a smile, these cats invite confidence

**AQUARIUS** — Somewhat aloof and superior, this is a rare and gifted cat

**CAPRICORN** — A well-disciplined cat who'd rather work hard than play hard

**SCORPIO** — A quiet cat with an affinity for the occult

**SAGITTARIUS** — Always ready to try something new

# THE DRAGON

**GEMINI** — Impulsive and creative, but has no "stick-to-itiveness"

**CANCER** — Quiet strength and regal calm typify this combination

**TAURUS** — A stubborn sort, this dragon is impossible to budge

**LEO** — A born leader whose immense power is almost frightening

**ARIES** — A sensitive, if somewhat aloof, dragon

**VIRGO** — A good-hearted, hard-working soul

**PISCES** — An artsy-craftsy type with lots of determination

**LIBRA** — Cut out for domestic life

**AQUARIUS** — Has an uncanny ability for mental telepathy

**SCORPIO** — A holy terror; would rather fight than do anything else

**CAPRICORN** — Needs to work hard to be appreciated

**SAGITTARIUS** — Ambitious and idealistic

# THE SNAKE

**GEMINI**
Will succeed as long as the job requires a glib tongue

**CANCER**
A good provider who likes to stay home

**TAURUS**
A born procrastinator

**LEO**
Quiet on the outside, seething on the inside

**ARIES**
This poor snake suffers from internal conflicts

**VIRGO**
A good soul who loves to do nice things for those he likes

**PISCES**
An overly sensitive snake who wallows in self pity

**LIBRA**
A vain sort who loves to be pampered

**AQUARIUS**
Not a very serious snake, but a very special one

**CAPRICORN**
These snakes are destined for greatness

**SAGITTARIUS**
A stubborn, opinionated snake, but a successful one

**SCORPIO**
A cynical snake who has little self esteem

# THE HORSE

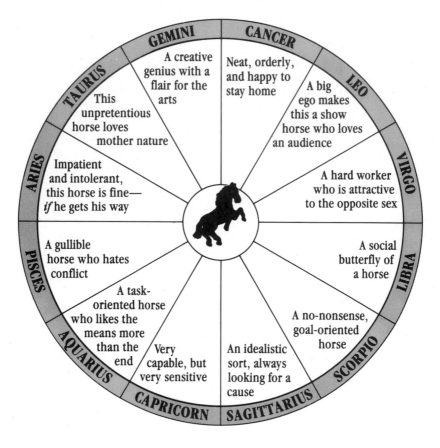

**GEMINI**
A creative genius with a flair for the arts

**CANCER**
Neat, orderly, and happy to stay home

**TAURUS**
This unpretentious horse loves mother nature

**LEO**
A big ego makes this a show horse who loves an audience

**ARIES**
Impatient and intolerant, this horse is fine— *if* he gets his way

**VIRGO**
A hard worker who is attractive to the opposite sex

**PISCES**
A gullible horse who hates conflict

**LIBRA**
A social butterfly of a horse

**AQUARIUS**
A task-oriented horse who likes the means more than the end

**CAPRICORN**
Very capable, but very sensitive

**SAGITTARIUS**
An idealistic sort, always looking for a cause

**SCORPIO**
A no-nonsense, goal-oriented horse

# THE GOAT

**GEMINI** — Quick-witted fun-lover who needs someone sober to guide him

**CANCER** — Can do anything he sets his mind to

**TAURUS** — This goat is his own worst enemy

**LEO** — Leo goats are good leaders

**ARIES** — Likes a good fight

**VIRGO** — A gullible goat who is easily disappointed

**PISCES** — A creative talent in search of an agent

**LIBRA** — Good with words, bad with money

**AQUARIUS** — Loves the arts, but needs prodding to participate

**SCORPIO** — A no-nonsense goat who demands his own way

**CAPRICORN** — A resourceful survivor

**SAGITTARIUS** — His brilliance comes out only if he feels safe

# THE MONKEY

**GEMINI** — Scatter-brained and hard to control

**CANCER** — An intense monkey who would make a good parent

**LEO** — Raw energy and lust for power combine here

**TAURUS** — Quick-witted and slow to anger

**VIRGO** — A sharp wit that cuts even himself

**ARIES** — A tough monkey—hard to dominate

**LIBRA** — This monkey makes great company—if you like someone who talks a lot

**PISCES** — A sense of humor tempers this monkey's sensitivity

**SCORPIO** — A highly creative, highly sexed, highly self-destructive monkey

**AQUARIUS** — Born to serve; has very high ideals

**SAGITTARIUS** — A smart monkey with integrity to boot

**CAPRICORN** — This monkey thrives on conflict

# THE ROOSTER

GEMINI — Wild mood swings

CANCER — Don't mistake his silent scheming for sloth

TAURUS — Full of cock and bull!

LEO — A prideful, showy sort

ARIES — An ego maniac with a strong sex drive

VIRGO — Fiercely principled; will die for his beliefs

PISCES — Blames self for everything

LIBRA — Inconsistent and impossible to predict

AQUARIUS — Insecurity makes this rooster hard to live with

SCORPIO — Refuses to grow up; easily provoked

CAPRICORN — This rooster just loves to travel

SAGITTARIUS — Your basic "do-gooder"

# *THE DOG*

**GEMINI** — A good, generous soul who is easily taken advantage of

**CANCER** — Emotional, sensitive; and giving

**TAURUS** — Austere on the surface, but loves a good bawdy joke

**LEO** — Loves to lead, hates to be made wrong

**ARIES** — Overly confident

**VIRGO** — A modest dog of high integrity

**PISCES** — A creative, sensitive soul who hates conflict

**LIBRA** — Likes harmony and will do anything to avoid conflict

**AQUARIUS** — Wants to help everyone all the time

**SCORPIO** — A cynical, vicious dog who will stop at nothing to get his way

**CAPRICORN** — A stoic sort with a heart of gold

**SAGITTARIUS** — A dog of action who is well meaning

# OFFICIAL ANIMAL HOROSCOPE FUTURE-PREDICTING CHART

Unlike western astrology, which requires you to consult the stars on a daily basis, Buddha thoughtfully worked things out so that with animal horoscopes you can plan the rest of your life at one sitting. Of course, you should train yourself to be alert to the dangers that are unique to your species, as well as to those opportunities to which you are particularly well suited. But beyond that, you need only to consult the following chart to be able to plan for a long, happy life.

To use this chart, locate your animal sign in the column on the left, then read across for each yearly prediction. Years that are particularly good for you are marked with ☺; bad years are marked with ⌒; and years that could go either way are marked with ⊖.

| YOUR SIGN | YEARS OF THE **PIG** | YEARS OF THE **RAT** | YEARS OF THE **BULL** | YEARS OF THE **TIGER** | YEARS OF THE **CAT** | YEARS OF THE **DRAGON** |
|---|---|---|---|---|---|---|
| PIG | ☺ A year of complete harmony and success | ⌢ A year of anxiety | ☺ A good year to start new business | ⌢ A bad year financially | ⊖ An okay year, but a good one for socializing | ☺ Smooth sailing; a good year at work |
| RAT | ⊖ A slow year; nothing exciting, either good or bad | ☺ A great year; success in all you do | ☺ Another good year, but not as good as the last | ⊖ An okay year, if you don't take risks | ⊖ A good year to be quiet and lay low | ☺ A very good year on all fronts |
| BULL | ☺ A good year, but only if you work at it | ☺ A good year, but success will be modest | ☺ Another nice year, particularly in your relationship with kids | ⌢ Everyone is down on you this year | ⊖ A slow year of recovery | ⊖ Continued slow recovery |
| TIGER | ⊖ Year starts out strong; but turns sour | ⌢ Bad luck all year | ⊖ A mixed year; lots of arguments | ⊖ An okay year, but not great | ☺ A happy, calm year | ⊖ A neutral year; okay, but not great |

| YEARS OF THE SNAKE | YEARS OF THE HORSE | YEARS OF THE GOAT | YEARS OF THE MONKEY | YEARS OF THE ROOSTER | YEARS OF THE DOG | YOUR SIGN |
|---|---|---|---|---|---|---|
| ⊖ A hectic year; bad for romance | ⌣ A good year, if you don't take big risks | ⊖ An okay year, but boring | ⌢ A troubled year | ⊖ A good year, if you work hard; bad if you don't | ⌢ Frustration abounds; don't count on "friends" | PIG |
| ⊖ A mixed year that ends better than it starts | ⌢ A long, hard year on all fronts | ⊖ Financial recovery, but love-life suffers | ⊖ A good year, but not by much | ⌣ A good year for new relationships | ⌢ Frustration and disappointment abound | RAT |
| ⌣ A great year; everything goes your way | ⊖ A let down after last year | ⌢ Bad, but not terrible | ⊖ You'll bounce back with a good financial year | ⌣ Continued success all year | ⊖ Anxiety rather than actual bad news makes this year mixed | BULL |
| ⊖ A continuation of last year | ⌣ A great year—the one you've been waiting for | ⊖ Good, but not as good as the last | ⌢ A long, trying year | ⊖ A moderately good year | ⊖ Nothing terrible, nothing great | TIGER |

| YOUR SIGN | YEARS OF THE PIG | YEARS OF THE RAT | YEARS OF THE BULL | YEARS OF THE TIGER | YEARS OF THE CAT | YEARS OF THE DRAGON |
|---|---|---|---|---|---|---|
| CAT | ⊖ A mixed year; don't be too optimistic | ⌣ A good year for calm, steady progress | ⊖ A tough year, but you'll survive | ⊖ Stay alert; carelessness could be fatal | ⌣ A year of complete harmony and success | ⊖ Mixed: good financially, but bad at home |
| DRAGON | ⌣ A return to normal after a bad year | ⌣ A good year to enjoy the good life | ⌣ Continued good luck | ⌢ Personal conflicts at work and home | ⊖ Calm returns; better year than the last | ⌣ A good year with fast progress on all fronts |
| SNAKE | ⊖ A year of great activity and chaos | ⊖ Continued activity, both good and bad | ⊖ A calmer, somewhat better year | ⊖ Lots of irritations, but only minor ones | ⊖ A busy, but rewarding year | ⊖ Despite lots of work, you won't advance much |
| HORSE | ⌢ Look for old investments to give you new headaches | ⌢ Bad year; avoid confrontations, especially legal ones | ⊖ Not a great year, but better than the last | ⌣ Quiet happiness all year | ⌣ A good year, especially financially | ⊖ A year to contemplate and plan |

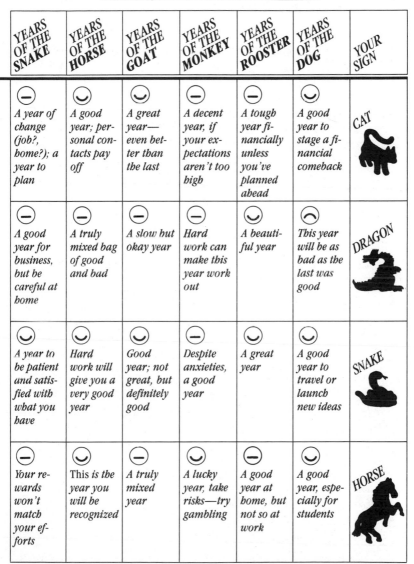

| YEARS OF THE SNAKE | YEARS OF THE HORSE | YEARS OF THE GOAT | YEARS OF THE MONKEY | YEARS OF THE ROOSTER | YEARS OF THE DOG | YOUR SIGN |
|---|---|---|---|---|---|---|
| ⊖ *A year of change (job?, home?); a year to plan* | ⌣ *A good year; personal contacts pay off* | ⌣ *A great year—even better than the last* | ⊖ *A decent year, if your expectations aren't too high* | ⊖ *A tough year financially unless you've planned ahead* | ⌣ *A good year to stage a financial comeback* | CAT |
| ⊖ *A good year for business, but be careful at home* | ⊖ *A truly mixed bag of good and bad* | ⊖ *A slow but okay year* | ⊖ *Hard work can make this year work out* | ⌣ *A beautiful year* | ⌢ *This year will be as bad as the last was good* | DRAGON |
| ⌣ *A year to be patient and satisfied with what you have* | ⌣ *Hard work will give you a very good year* | ⌣ *Good year; not great, but definitely good* | ⊖ *Despite anxieties, a good year* | ⌣ *A great year* | ⌣ *A good year to travel or launch new ideas* | SNAKE |
| ⊖ *Your rewards won't match your efforts* | ⌣ *This is the year you will be recognized* | ⊖ *A truly mixed year* | ⌣ *A lucky year, take risks—try gambling* | ⊖ *A good year at home, but not so at work* | ⌣ *A good year, especially for students* | HORSE |

| YOUR SIGN | YEARS OF THE PIG | YEARS OF THE RAT | YEARS OF THE BULL | YEARS OF THE TIGER | YEARS OF THE CAT | YEARS OF THE DRAGON |
|---|---|---|---|---|---|---|
| **GOAT** | ⊖ A fair year; one of recovery | ☺ A lucky year; try entering lotteries | ⌢ A long year full of quarrels | ⊖ A busy year with both good and bad times | ⊖ On balance, a good year; beware of physical injuries | ⊖ Lots of hard work; do not gamble this year |
| **MONKEY** | ⊖ Your rewards won't match your efforts | ☺ Lots of good luck and prosperity | ⊖ A year to be patient; a good year at home | ⊖ Exercise extreme caution to avoid a disasterous year | ☺ Prosperity time; a good year to change jobs | ☺ A good year for intangible gain |
| **ROOSTER** | ⌢ Lots of news, all of it bad; be patient | ⌢ Another bad year, physically and financially | ☺ A year of peaceful recuperation | ⊖ An uneventful, boring year at best | ⊖ More good than bad, but not great | ☺ A great year; success in all you do |
| **DOG** | ⊖ A calm year; hard work will make it a good one | ☺ A very good year across the board | ⊖ An axious year, but it turns out fine | ⊖ An uneventful year; be patient | ⊖ A good year, but only if you work at it | ⌢ You'll have to struggle just to survive |

| YEARS OF THE SNAKE | YEARS OF THE HORSE | YEARS OF THE GOAT | YEARS OF THE MONKEY | YEARS OF THE ROOSTER | YEARS OF THE DOG | YOUR SIGN |
|---|---|---|---|---|---|---|
| ☺ A good year; everybody likes you this year | ⊖ Despite minor illness, a good year | ⊖ Be practical and patient this year | ☺ A good year to advance at work | ☺ A good year, but an expensive one | ⌢ A nasty year full of upheaval and chaos | GOAT |
| ⊖ A year to be patient | ⊖ A frustrating year as you must remain patient | ⊖ A hectic year of ups and downs | ☺ A great year to start your own business | ⊖ A moderate year; beware of your competitors | ⌢ A bad year; people will renege on deals | MONKEY |
| ☺ Another good year | ⊖ A trying year—you're spoiled! | ☺ A safe, good year | ⊖ Anxieties could cloud your judgment; be careful | ⊖ A good, but not great year | ☺ A nice year, especially from a social standpoint | ROOSTER |
| ☺ Hard work pays off | ⊖ Rewards will be in proportion to work | ⊖ Anxieties keep you from enjoying life | ⊖ Another fair, but good year | ⊖ Anxieties cause self doubt | ☺ A calm, essentially good year | DOG |